Adrian
Whiteh...

C000214993

The Witney District

IN OLD PHOTOGRAPHS

Best Wishes

Tom Worley

The Witney District

IN OLD PHOTOGRAPHS

Collected by TOM WORLEY

Alan Sutton Publishing Limited
Phoenix Mill · Far Thrupp
Stroud · Gloucestershire

First published 1992

Copyright © Tom Worley, 1992

**British Library Cataloguing
in Publication Data**

Worley, Tom
  Witney District in Old Photographs
  I. Title
  942.571

ISBN 0–7509–0174–8

Typeset in 9/10 Sabon.
Typesetting and origination by
Alan Sutton Publishing Limited.
Printed in Great Britain by
WBC Print Ltd, Bridgend.

Contents

Mrs Amelia Carter, benefactress to the villages of Kencot, Filkins, Clanfield and Bampton. She provided recreational and reading room facilities for the young men, to keep them away from the demon drink. Her will was approved in 1902. She is shown here in a Shakespearian pose that Miss Ellen Terry would have approved of.

Introduction

As a follow-up to *Witney in Old Photographs*, this book attempts to show a representative selection of pictures of the surrounding district. The area covered is roughly from Filkins in the west to Eynsham in the east, and Shipton and Charlbury in the north to Clanfield and Bampton in the south. It was with considerable difficulty that pictures were located in each of the communities covered in the book, but the task was eased by the owners' willingness to lend their photographs for copying, and their enthusiasm in giving the information which has made this book possible. I gratefully acknowledge this assistance and a list of names appears at the end of the book as a token of my gratitude.

One of the most pleasant aspects of the research has been the opportunity to meet people and visit what must be one of the prettiest areas in the whole country. I have viewed places which I thought I knew from a fresh angle and had the opportunity to compare pictures of yesteryear with today's scene, and marvelled at the skill and ingenuity of people who have converted what once had been a semi-derelict hovel into a most desirable residence. I have seen the stark contrast between now and then in working and living conditions and I realize that it was not too long ago that people lived in dark, damp and draughty houses. We take for granted such things as electricity, wholesome pure piped water, indoor toilets, baths and central heating. However, I do approve of the slower pace at which the people lived; we are all in too big a hurry, and with so many cars on our roads we have forgotten the pleasure of walking.

I have found several interesting facts during research. For example, a man drafted into the forces found someone willing to go in his place, and I have seen his certificate of exemption. During the summer months men from the area would go to London, taking their scythes to mow the parks; on the way home they would work at places like Windsor and be paid off on reaching Oxford. If hospitalized they were given a certificate to say they were not able to follow their usual employment, which was overstamped in bold letters: 'Not to be used for begging'. At Filkins annual club dinner in 1904, the butcher's account was for 219 lb of mixed beef, pork, lamb, and ham at eight pence per pound. The total bill came to £7 6s.

Here is a selection from a school logbook. An entry dated 1880 records that a girl started school aged one year eleven months. In December 1916 the classroom temperature registered 40°F; perhaps the First World War had something to do with it. The head teacher's salary in 1883 was £7 10s for three months' work. Several entries recorded the caning of boys for truancy and impudence. The school had to close on several occasions because of scarlet fever, whooping cough, measles, diphtheria, and ringworm, and the district nurse visited regularly, usually for dirty heads (lice).

It was very revealing to peruse the Witney workhouse entries register for 1839–41 which covers roughly the parishes dealt with by this book. Quite a lot of children therein were just babes in arms, and children reaching the age of 13 would have their names removed from the register, presumably for the girls to go into service and the boys to work on farms or in factories. Some of the entries were for whole families: father, mother and several children.

It could be said by people who have lived in the villages all their lives: 'What does he know about our village?' I only know what they have told me, what I have found in the libraries and archives, and what is written on the backs of the pictures, so it is a good question and I beg forgiveness for any mistakes which might have crept in.

When I set out to produce this book I was concerned that I might not find enough material. I should not have worried, because the few villages where I failed to find material were more than compensated for by the others. In the end I had so many pictures that my problem was selecting the ones to use and rejecting the hundreds of equally interesting and worthy photographs.

For the convenience of the reader I have divided the book into sections, each being a group of villages in the same area.

I have enjoyed delving into the pictorial history of the area around Witney and if the reader gets as much pleasure from the book as I have had in its production, my labour will be amply rewarded.

SECTION ONE

Alvescot – Clanfield – Filkins
Broadwell – Kencot – Langford

Alvescot village in 1906. The lean-to on the end of the house has since been removed and houses built on the site to the right of the picture.

A baptism in the mill pool at Alvescot in around 1900.

Alvescot, showing the Red Lion public house and village shop. This postcard is dated 2 June 1926.

Clanfield in 1930, showing the stream which runs through the village on the right and Clare's village stores on the left.

The Carter Institute at Clanfield. This was a gift to the village from Mrs Amelia Carter, a benefactress, as a refuge for young boys from the evils of alcoholic beverages. Her will was approved in 1902 so this picture probably dates from about 1900.

Clanfield Methodist church jubilee celebrations on 18 July 1959, with the Revd L.T. Smith, the minister, and the Revd Oxley, the vicar of Clanfield presiding. This was the original Nonconformist meeting house and is no longer in use.

Thames Valley Ironworks Band (from Knapps iron foundry) in around 1905. The band played on Clanfield village green on Sunday evenings. Knapps made agricultural implements, including drills and hay loaders.

Knapps Thames Valley Ironworks Band poses outside the owner's house in around 1913.

Clanfield Wesleyan chapel holds its bazaar at Green Close in front of Miss Balgrove's house in 1868.

There was always plenty of work for craftsmen in Clanfield. Left to right: F. and R. Baston, carpenters; W.L. Hicks, farrier; F.L. Lawrence, a striker at the forge in Bampton Road, in around 1930.

Clanfield bridge, with the Masons Arms public house in the centre and Mr Clarke's fish and chip shop to the right in around 1904. Clarke also repaired shoes.

George Swinford of Filkins was born in 1887, worked as a stonemason and lived to be one hundred. He is displaying an easel which was used by William Morris the artist, poet and social reformer. Mr Swinford founded the village museum, which was opened in 1931 by the Rt Hon. Herbert Morrison MP.

The upper class of Filkins Church of England School in 1909. The school had 108 pupils. Mrs Robert Giles, left, and Mrs Ivy Dore, right, were the teachers. The children of the village now go to Langford School until they are eleven and then transfer to Burford Comprehensive School. The building is now used by a play group.

A Filkins School group displays some of the tools of their non-academic activities on 12 February 1908. Mr Frederick Dawson is the master.

Filkins Hall after the fire of 1876. It was the home of the Colston family in the mid-nineteenth century. They were a philanthropic family with schools and the Colston Hall in Bristol named after them. The house was rebuilt and a recent resident was Sir William Goodenough.

Lower End, Broadwell, in August 1907.

Broadwell village shop and post office in 1909.

Kencott Manor House in April 1907. Later it was the home of Major-General Abraham.

Richard and Lucy Dossett, who were residents of Kencott between 1800 and 1853. The picture is dated 1840. Their son George was a baker and William Morris was one of his customers.

Langford war memorial. This was a parade to commemorate its unveiling and dedication in 1919.

Langford shop and post office in 1919.

The Nonconformist chapel at Langford in 1919. It is now used as a surgery.

SECTION TWO

Shilton – Carterton – Bampton
Black Bourton – Brize Norton
Aston – Cote

The Shill brook, which flows through Shilton, with its bridge and bridge house, on 8 August 1906.

Shilton church and school at the top of the hill on the left, seen from Short Edge.

Shilton in 1928. The village was very tidy and pretty, with well maintained houses and trim gardens. Most of the trees are no longer there and the corner has been redeveloped. The pond is on the right.

The centre of Shilton in around 1911, with the Rose and Crown public house in the centre and the small shop on the extreme right behind the bicycle.

Straight Hill, Shilton. The elm trees were cut down in the 1920s or '30s.

Shilton, in October 1908, showing cottages at the top of Bridge Street near the crossroads. The building on the right was once the post office.

Shilton School shortly after it was erected in 1864.

Shilton Church of England School group in 1923. Pupils of all ages were educated in one room, which was divided into two by a glass partition.

Charles William Maisey of Shilton on 3 November 1910. Maisey had a distinguished careeer at sea and the photograph was taken in Genoa when he was captain of the SS *Craigearn*.

HMS *Worcester*, a cadet training vessel at Greenhithe on the Thames near Dartford. The captain was C.W. Maisey from Shilton. He died in 1924 and there is a memorial to him in Shilton church.

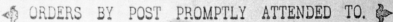

EDWIN GARDNER,

APPLE GRINDER,

SHILTON,

BAMPTON, OXON,

Begs to thank the public for their previous patronage, and to inform them that he still carries on the above business, and trusts by strict attention to the same, to merit a continuance of their favours.

ORDERS BY POST PROMPTLY ATTENDED TO.

Edwin Gardner of Shilton would take his horse-drawn apple crusher to clients who had crops of apples for cider-making.

Edwin Gardner, left, and Harry Gardner, facing him, at work with their apple (cider) press, in about 1890. It took two horses to turn the screw of the press.

Frank Gardner the baker delivering in Shilton in around 1911. Gardner lived from 1874 until 1957.

The Brize Norton road at Carterton in around 1904. The crossroads is off the picture to the left.

William Carter, the chairman of Homesteads Ltd, and founder of Carterton.

In 1894, the 740 acre Rock Farm was in the parish of Black Bourton, and was sold by the Duke of Marlborough to Thomas Arkell for £5,450. In 1901 he sold it on to William Carter for £8,880, who divided it into about 350 plots, selling them at between £20 and £35 an acre and naming the settlement Carterton. By September 1902, the settlers had built sixteen houses, most of the new residents becoming market gardeners specializing in tomatoes and poultry. The first school was opened in 1928; by 1932 the population had grown to 504 and there were 194 houses. In September 1937 an RAF station was opened and this encouraged the gradual expansion of Carterton. After the return of the RAF following the Second World War and around fifteen years during which time the USAAF was resident, many houses were built for servicemen. From that time onward there has been a very large private house building programme and the population today is fast approaching 15,000. The next few years will probably see great changes to the central shopping area.

Burford Road, Carterton, in around 1904, with the entrance to Arkell Avenue on the left, and Mr Baldwin's house on the right. The next building is believed to be the first Co-operative shop, which later moved to the crossroads site.

The old original Lodge for Rock Farm House Burford Road.

Rock Farm Lodge, on the corner of Arkell Avenue, in around 1908. Rock Farm is believed to have got its name because of the amount of free stone available on the site.

Mr J. Garner purchased a plot of 4½ acres in June 1902 from William Carter for £97 10s. This is the dwelling that he built on the Black Bourton road.

Mr Gallager's shop at Carterton crossroads. Gallager opened for business on August Bank Holiday 1902, having brought all his furniture and shop stock from Scotland in a horse-drawn vehicle.

Carterton Horticultural Society in around 1930. Back row, left to right: Messrs Lucas, Hamer, Smith, Butler, Watson, Jackson, Jones, Rose, Southam, Ball, Moss, Horne. Front row: Messrs Helman, Burge, Winstone, Ritchens, Wm Goodenough (president), Foulder, Rose, Blunt, Yeats.

Mr and Mrs Henry Woodbridge in their smart pony-drawn trap at Aston in December 1913.

Before William Carter bought Rock Farm, the whole area was part of the parish of Black Bourton and the postal address was Black Bourton, Faringdon, Berkshire. Revd Pinder was the vicar of the enlarged area which included all the land which was to become Carterton. Pinder is seen here at his wedding to Miss Neate of Alvescot rectory in 1913.

The Carpenters Arms (known locally as 'The Axe'), at the southern end of Brize Norton, in 1905. It ceased trading in 1992.

Brize Norton, showing Bognor Terrace in the middle of the village, in 1905.

St Britius church, partly hidden by a neatly thatched cottage, in 1905.

Brize Norton, looking south from the church, in 1905.

Brize Norton general stores, near the church, in July 1905. On 24 July 1873 this business and dwelling was sold at auction for £300. Included in the sale was the shop with a three-bedroom house, three attics, a bakehouse, brewhouse, baconhouse, flour room, stores, yard, garden and large orchard of about an acre.

The middle of Brize Norton, from a postcard dated 6 January 1907. Farm workers with their carts and horses stop at The Chequers public house.

Wally Barnett from Alvescot and the girls he transported from Brize Norton Church of England School on their Friday trip to Bampton for cookery lessons, 1927. Back row, left to right: Lucy and Eva Fields, Phyllis Badger, Dora Drinkwater, Janet Timms, Edie Archer, Iris Preston, ? Kyte. Front row: Elsie Ashby, Vera Faulkner, May Parker, Marjorie Jones, Sylvia Townsend.

Brize Norton Mothers Union, with the Revd Sturgess, ready for an outing to Cheltenham in June 1920.

The fashions are worth a second look in this group of Brize Norton Mothers Union members on their summer outing in the early 1920s.

The Brize Norton Band pose outside the Primitive Methodist church. Standing, left to right: Fred Field, Tom Winfield, C. Wilkins, ? Holtom, George Faulkner, ? Calibfield. Seated: -?-, William Faulkner, ? Timms, Tom Bye, Bert Faulkner, Arthur Bellinger.

The vicar and choir of St Britius church, Brize Norton. The date is not known, but it is before 1884 because John Worley, the churchwarden (in top hat), died then.

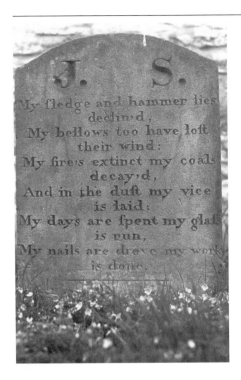

My fledge and hammer lies
declin'd,
My bellows too have lost
their wind:
My fire's extinct my coals
decay'd,
And in the duft my vice
is laid:
My days are fpent my glafs
is run,
My nails are drove my work
is done.

An unusual epitaph in Brize Norton church burial ground in memory of John Silman (1772–1836), the village blacksmith.

This sale notice on behalf of the executors of Thomas Silman on 6 April 1875 realized the following amounts:

- Lot one. Four stone cottages and outbuildings. Sold for £242 10s.
- Lot two. Three stone cottages, gardens and outbuildings. Sold for £165.
- Lot three. Garden land with fruit trees and a stream of water, let for £14 per annum, about ½ mile from Bampton station. Sold for £260.

BRIZE NORTON.
FREEHOLD COTTAGE
PROPERTY
AND
GARDEN LAND.
TO BE SOLD BY AUCTION, BY
MR. LONG,
AT THE CHEQUERS INN, BRIZENORTON,
On Tuesday, April 6th, 1875,
AT FIVE O'CLOCK, P.M.

Under Conditions to be then produced, by order of the Trustees of the Will of Thomas Silman, deceased:—

7 Stone-built and Slated TENEMENTS, and 2 Acres of Rich GARDEN and ORCHARD LAND.

LOT ONE.—Four recently-erected Stone-built and Slated COTTAGES, with Out-buildings and Yard, situate in Brizenorton, in the respective occupations of JAMES UPSTONE, THOMAS TIMMS, WILLIAM ___ and WILLIAM POWLER.

LOT TWO.—Three Stone-built and Slated COTTAGES, with Gardens and Out-buildings, in Brizenorton, in the occupations of JOSEPH HUNT, JOHN MILLS, and EDWARD MILLS.

LOT THREE. ___ GARDEN LAND, with full bearing FRUIT TREES and ___ WATER, containing ___ 0P., in the occupation of Mr. JOSEPH ALLIS, at a Rental of £14 6s. 0d. per Annum, situate in Brizenorton, and about Half a mile from the Bampton Station of the East Gloucestershire Railway.

To view the Property apply ___ and for particulars to Mr. ___ the ___ , ___ Auctioneer, Long ___ , Solicitors ___ the Auctioneer, Witney.

Charles Wilkins, the Brize Norton carrier, with his wife, Martha, and daughter, Annie, in about 1908. He was the Brize Norton carrier to Oxford via Witney, taking eggs and other produce from the farms to Oxford and bringing back supplies, including meat, and the Oxford newspapers.

Entering Bampton from the direction of Brize Norton, in around 1900. It is interesting to see trees growing in the middle of what is now a very busy road.

Bampton Market Square in around 1910. The Talbot Inn, in the background on the right, is believed to have been named after a family of that name that lived at Bampton Castle.

Broad Street, Bampton, or the 'Broadway' as it was sometimes called, in around 1900. The gateway into the manor, centre background, was closed many years ago, and a new entry made round the corner.

Bampton Market Square: a peaceful scene when compared with today.

This butchers shop, shown here in 1903, faced the town committee rooms in the centre of the square at Bampton. A sign outside advertised 'cheap butcher'. The building to the right, probably the butcher's house, was pulled down and the hall used by the Women's Institute was built on the site.

The Eagle public house, Bampton, in around 1900. It was converted into a private house in the spring of 1992, and is now known as Eagle House.

Bampton, with the Grange on the right, looking towards the Aston and Buckland roads, in around 1900.

Bridge Street, Bampton, in around 1911. The Elephant and Castle public house is on the left. The original postcard was printed in Berlin.

Bampton Grammar School in 1840. It is now used as the library extension.

Fête day at Bampton in around 1915, with children playing games on Ernest Gerring's College Farm.

The band assembled under a banner proclaiming 'Go thou and do likewise' outside the church of St Mary the Virgin, Bampton, in 1905.

The Square and war memorial, Aston, in the early 1920s. Long's grocery shop is on the left; today it is the post office. Jones's meat and grocery shop is on the right. The thatched cottages on the right have been pulled down and replaced with a modern house.

Aston House, the Baptist manse, situated next door to the chapel. The thatched cottage is no longer there. The roads and pavements were not made up in this picture, dated 7 December 1917.

The entrance to Back Lane, Aston, on 3 August 1917. Here also the roads and pavements are not made up.

The name Long has been associated with Aston for many years. The family have been grocers and provision merchants, carpenters, undertakers and wheelwrights, and for many years ran the post office.

Club day at Aston, 1910. A day to celebrate, when money paid into a savings club was drawn out and villagers put on their best clothes to go to hear the band.

With two barrels of beer the men of Aston were intent on a merry trip to Southsea some time in the late 1920s.

The Aston Laundry and staff in around 1937. Back row, left to right: John Stone (engineer), Cissie Redman, Mrs Wells, Ms Sparrowhawk, Mrs Beechey, Mrs Ball, -?-, Molly Johnson, E. Spurrett, -?-, Louie Fitchett, -?-, Win Beechey, Teddy Taylor. Middle row: Murial Townsend, Mrs Johnson, Mr Cruley (proprietor), Mr Armstrong (manager), Eileen Dix. Front row: -?-, Alma and Brenda Shewry, -?-, Lily Clack, Cissie Sparrowhawk.

Ten Spanish refugee children at Aston in 1938 with their mentor, Miss Phyllis Ransom. When General Franco was advancing on Bilbao during the Spanish Civil War, a number of children were rescued from the streets of the city and brought by British warship to England. They did not know what their fate would be and some thought they had been taken prisoner. The children, none of whom could speak English, were dispersed through-out the country and this group came to St Joseph's, Aston. A local committee, consisting mainly of the wives of professionals and businessmen, was set up to care for them, and the children chose one of its number to be their guardian and honorary parent. They settled in well with the help of a student of Spanish from Oxford University and were later joined by a Spanish teacher.

Four wheelwrights who worked for Mr Long at Aston. The faggots in the rear were fired to heat the metal rims for fitting on wooden cart weels. Left to right: Ernest Long, Harry Glenister, Richard Long, Will Johnson.

Aston Church of England School group of 5 to 14 year olds in around 1931. Back row, left to right: K. Taylor, J. Barton, J. Sparrowhawk, -?-, -?-, F. Florey, Miss P. Wheale. Middle row: H. Long, -?-, I. Gotobed, D. Wells, Q. Winterbourne, K. Sparrowhawk, D. Brooks, T. Dewe. Front row: I. Bishop, -?-, J. Taylor, R. Hewer, M. Hayden, K. Harris, M. Panting.

Carpenters, blacksmiths and wheelwrights who worked for Mr Aubrey Long at Aston, in around 1947.

Aston Baptist Sunday School outing to Southsea on 10 August 1937. Two of Mr Oliver's coaches took the party.

Aston manse. Mrs and Miss Blackaby on the right are the wife and daughter of the minister.

Cote Baptist chapel interior. It is thought that it was built during the period of the 'five mile act' when Nonconformist churches were not permitted within five miles of a town. It is probably one of the oldest Protestant churches in the country. The old box pews are worthy of a visit.

SECTION THREE

Eynsham – Stanton Harcourt – Sutton
Newbridge – Northmoor
Bablock Hythe – Standlake

Queen Street Eynsham, showing the Queen's Head public house in the centre of the picture, in April 1907.

Station Road, Eynsham, in 1906. As there has not been a railway track through Eynsham since the Beeching decision to close the branch line from Yarnton to Fairford in 1970, it is likely that not many people will recognize this scene. The building on the left is a railway company house, probably used by the crossing keeper.

The Square, Eynsham, September 1906.

Bartholomew Rooms in the Market Square, Eynsham, in June 1906. The upper storey over the years has housed the Bartholomew School and the Roman Catholic church. The ground floor was at one time the lock-up. Like most lock-ups of the period it was probably used mostly to confine drunks overnight.

The house between St Leonard's church and the Red Lion public house which appears in this 1906 picture was subsequently pulled down and the war memorial now occupies the site.

The interior of St Leonard's church in 1909, showing the candle chandelier in the centre and the old gas lamps on each side of the nave. The church was renovated in the 1980s and an electronic organ installed.

Cassington Mill in July 1906. The mill was last used for grinding corn in 1938. A mill at Cassington was registered in the Domesday Book around 1085. At one time there was a tithe of 175 eels payable to the church. The mill was known as a sack-and-a-half mill, because it produced one-and-a-half sacks of flour weighing $2\frac{1}{2}$ cwt each hour.

The Talbot Inn, Eynsham, in May 1906. The Limb and the Chil brooks join nearby and flow past on the right of the inn, where there was a wharf for barge traffic. In the 1930s a sugar-beet factory was built at the rear.

The cross at Eynsham as it was on 24 December 1908. It dates back to about 1350. It was removed and rebuilt with new stone in 1991 because of its poor state of repair.

The Board School, Eynsham, in July 1908. It is still in use as part of the newer Bartholomew Comprehensive School at the rear. The Board School was under the control of a board (or committee) in accordance with the 1870 elementary education legislation.

Swinford toll-bridge over the River Thames. It was built by Lord Abingdon in 1769, and an act of George III's parliament permitted tolls to be collected. Today the toll is merely an inconvenience but at one time the fee was punitive.

Stanton Harcourt, showing the stocks on the left, in the early 1900s. The cottage on the left has gone and the site has been redeveloped.

Stanton Harcourt on 5 July 1906. Following a fire in around 1943, the row of cottages known as All Souls now has tiled roofs.

Stanton Harcourt. The end of the village on the Standlake road. The original is a postcard with a King Edward VII stamp, so it dates to about 1904.

The Harcourt Arms at Stanton Harcourt in 1907 when it was just a small country pub. The horse and cart on the right is from Beard Mill just outside the village.

The centre of Stanton Harcourt in 1904, with John Aker's bakery and grocery shop on the left. In the background is the old dovecote and the entrance to the parsonage.

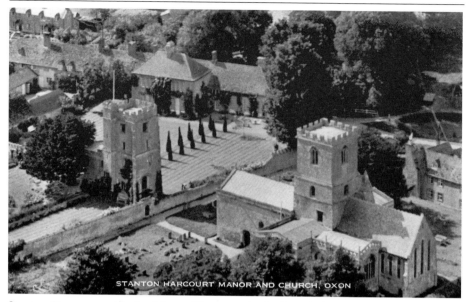

Stanton Harcourt, with the Manor House at the back and the church in the right foreground. The other castellated building is Pope's Tower, where Alexander Pope spent a few years in the early 1700s in order to finish his translation of Homer in peaceful and quiet surroundings.

The Ancient Order of Foresters head the parade on club day at Stanton Harcourt, in 1912. Its banner says 'Court Welcome No. 6686 A.O. Foresters'.

Stanton Harcourt Church of England School group.

Stanton Harcourt School group in 1909. The school closed in 1948 and pupils now attend a new school until they are eleven, when they transfer to Bartholomew School, Eynsham.

Stanton Harcourt Women's Institute outing in about 1917. The bus had a 12 m.p.h. speed limit.

Harvest time at Beaumonts Farm, Sutton, in about 1930. Left to right: Arthur Trinder, Bob Coles, Arthur Barnett, Billy Batts. Standing on the cart: Jimmy Green.

The *Rose Revived* on the River Thames at Newbridge.

A gated road at Lower End, Sutton, in around 1900.

The Maybush public house at Newbridge on the River Thames.

The Wesleyan Home Mission car regularly toured the area preaching the gospel at the beginning of this century.

Northmoor church.

Northmoor lock. John Wesley frequently had to cross the Thames on his preaching tours. In 1764 he had a hazardous crossing on his way to Witney, but it is thought that the crossing would have been made near Eynsham, probably where the toll-bridge is now situated.

The Chequers Inn and ferryboat at Bablock Hythe on the River Thames, in around 1910. The ferry was a short-cut from Standlake and Stanton Harcourt to Cumnor and Oxford.

This picture shows Mr J. Douglas, the Standlake carrier, taking his horse and wagon across the Thames on the ferryboat, on his way home from Oxford. The whole area fell into disrepair until recently, when after complete renovation and modernization the public house reopened in 1992 as the Ferryman Inn.

Standlake just after the First World War, celebrating peace with a fancy dress parade.

Another glimpse of the Standlake peace celebrations in around 1919.

Mr J. Douglas, the Standlake carrier, in around 1900.

The Douglas family kept the Standlake village stores. Here we see Frank (centre), in around 1922, unloading sacks of sugar and soda which he had just collected from the goods yard of Witney railway station on his horse-drawn brewer's cart.

SECTION FOUR

Witney Aerodrome – Cogges
Ducklington – Hardwick
South Leigh

Witney aerodrome, which was used during the First World War for pilot training, was sold by auction when war ended. Witney and Oxford Aero Club were in occupation during the 1930s, starting a pilot and engineer training course in 1932.

A Witney and Oxford Aero Club plane.

The clubhouse of Witney and Oxford Aero Club, which was opened at a garden party on 8 June 1935. The Duchess of Bedford flew in from Woburn to perform the official opening.

The messroom cum lounge of the aero club. Another official opening took place on 18 July 1937 of the new residential mess by the Rt Hon. Lord Sherbourne DSO, for the Witney Aeronautical College.

This mobile steam engine was used to power various farm machines at Mr Mawles' farm at Cogges. The farm is now the Cogges Farm Museum under the control of the County Council.

The children of Cogges School in fancy dress, probably for the Witney pageant, in 1936. Back row, left to right: M. Hatton, E. Smith, J. Miles. Middle row: -?-, E. Hughes, H. Bull, J. Rapley, W. Townsend, P. Bridgeman, K. Foster, B. Kearsey, E. Surman, B. Basson. Front row: P. Smith, K. Hester, M. Hughes, R. Godfrey, E. Maycock.

Cogges Church of England Primary School in 1932. Back row, left to right: E. Smith, T. Taylor, T. Brogden, S. Bridgeman, D. Strong. Middle row: W. Surman, M. Beale, D. Glaister, K. Buckingham, R. Woodcock, C. Bridgeman, D. Pimm, S. Harris. Front row: M. Dore, K. Hester, J. Bridgeman, D. Bishop, W. Townsend, F. Woodcock, K. Foster. Miss Rowlands is the teacher.

Cogges School group, in around 1970, with their teacher, Miss Pat Lakin.

Cogges church and vicarage, which are near to Manor Farm, which was taken over by the County Council and turned into a farm museum.

Cogges schoolchildren in the summer of 1936. The occasion is not known, but one boy holds the Bishop's Prize. The school was under the wing of the vicar of Cogges and he frequently visited the school to conduct religious instruction.

The approach road to Ducklington from Witney in around 1920.

Ducklington pond, school and church, in 1909. Out of the picture to the left is a large oak tree, alas now dying. It was planted on 9 August 1902 to commemorate the coronation of King Edward VII.

Ducklington pond in June 1911. In the corner of the churchyard nearest to the pond is an oak tree grown from an acorn from the oak mentioned on page 79. It was planted by a 14-year-old schoolboy, John Stone, to commemorate King George V's coronation.

Ducklington, looking towards the rectory, in 1909.

Schoolboys and their master pose outside the church.

Ducklington Church of England School group in around 1924.

Ducklington scout troop. Charles Woolford and Jack Burton were scoutmasters for a few years.

Dr McCray, the rector of Ducklington, and his daughter with the church choir.

The children of Ducklington celebrate, in around 1946. The occasion is not known but is believed to be a celebration of the end of the Second World War.

It is well worth a visit to South Leigh church to see the frescoes on the walls. This picture was taken on 7 May 1904. In 1725 John Wesley preached his first sermon in this church. A programme of restoration was completed in 1992.

Scouts and cubs from Hammersmith, under their scoutmaster William Brind and his wife Lily, used to erect the tents for the summer camp at Hardwick. This picture was taken in the 1930s.

Scouts and cubs at Hardwick in the 1930s, enjoying the river and fresh air. For some this would have been their first holiday outside London. On the way home they would always visit friends at Sutton.

SECTION FIVE

Hailey – North Leigh – Ramsden
Eynsham Hall – New Yatt

Poffley End, Hailey, in around 1900.

Mary Ann Harris stands opposite the pond at Poffley End, Hailey, which overflowed after heavy rain, flooding the cottages. The pond has since been filled and the verge grassed over. This photograph was taken in around 1900.

Poffley End, Hailey, in around 1900. The house on the right is named the Old Manor House and is one of the oldest in Hailey.

Poffley End Farm, Hailey, in 1925. Ricks used to be built by placing wood and faggots across staddle stones, after which the sheafs of corn were put into place as shown. Finally the rick was thatched to keep the rain out. Raising a rick helped keep it dry and the rats out.

Middletown, Hailey, in around 1900. The ivy-clad house later became the post office and is now a private house.

Middletown, Hailey, in around 1920. The new St John the Evangelist church is sited behind the war memorial, with the Methodist chapel in the background.

The house on the extreme left in this photograph from around 1900 is the one shown on page 88.

Hailey fair outside the Carpenters Arms public house. It is all part of the club day celebrations, which included a dinner. This postcard is dated 22 August 1910.

St John's church in Hailey was consecrated in 1761 and demolished in 1868, shortly after this photograph was taken. It was replaced by the present St John the Evangelist church on a new site. The building started in 1866 to a design of Clapton Crabbe Rolfe, a son of the rector, and the church was consecrated on 26 April 1869.

The Revd George Crabbe Rolfe (1839–93), incumbent of Hailey church, with his family.

Laying the foundation stone of Hailey Nonconformist chapel in 1908. The building has been used for residential purposes for some years.

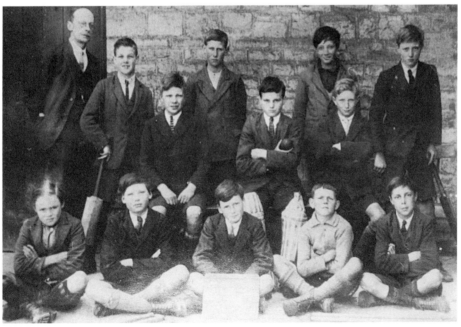
Hailey School cricket team with their master, Mr Joseph Wyatt, in around 1924. Wyatt was a good teacher with a reputation for strict discipline.

Hailey cricket team, cup winners 1930/1. Standing, left to right: E. Robinson, R. Groves, C. Rose, H. Goves, T. Pratley, W. Groves. Middle row: P. Hill, R. Buckingham, L. Clements, H. Goves, P. Beale, Front row: J. Fisher, J. Pickett.

Hailey Jubilee Committee in 1935. Back row, left to right: J. Buckingham, P. Buckingham, F. Strong, F. Masters, F. Wyatt, J. Telling, N. Phipps, G. Thornett, R. Blake, A. Preston, A. Luckett, H. Dyer, C. Hickman, D. Jones, T. Harris. Front row: Mrs P. Buckingham, Mrs A. Townsend, Mrs D. Jones, Mrs J. Nash, Mrs F. Strong, Mrs J. Telling, Mrs E. Buckingham, Mrs J. Smith, Mrs A. Luckett, Mrs F. Wyatt, Mrs N. Phipps, Mrs J. Clements, Mrs M. Buckingham, Mrs G. Clements. The photograph was taken in the church field behind the old Carpenters Arms public house.

North Leigh windmill and pond as seen from Cuckamus Green. Unfortunately the windmill was allowed to fall into disrepair. However, the top has now been capped to keep the weather out.

The Masons Arms public house, North Leigh, in the 1920s.

Mr Arkell, the North Leigh carrier, in the 1930s. His main runs were to Oxford and Witney, carrying passengers and goods. When the bus companies included the villages on the routes that they served, the role of the carrier declined.

Repairs to the Witney–Hanborough road outside the north lodge gate of Eynsham Hall, North Leigh, in around 1938–9. The roller driver is Fred Wickson and other men include Fred Hazel, Tuard Lay and two Dix brothers.

The two pictures on this page show the number of men needed to bring in the harvest. During August there would be absenteeism at the schools, with children helping in the fields, often causing teachers to start the summer holidays early.

After the crops had been harvested, mobile chicken houses would be taken to the fields so that hens could scratch for grain in the stubble.

The Revd Harding, vicar of St Mary's church, North Leigh, and Dorothy Hopkins, the organist, with the choristers in the mid-1950s.

North Leigh School group in 1920. Back row, left to right: G. Arkell, F. Willis, W. Willis, B. Brown, R. Goodman, F. Baston, M. Hill, -?-, -?-, W. Claridge, M. Smith. Middle row: F. Porter, H. Simister, R. Tibbetts, W. Long, W. Breakspeare, -?-, A. Pratley, R. Judd, T. Hazell, W. Cooper, M. Woodward. Front row: -?-, G. Hazell, E. Cooper, -?-, T. Arkell, E. Langford, W. Bishop, O. Hicks, E. Cooper, V. Breakspeare, E. Green, E. Cambourne, -?-, W. Partlett, W. Wickson.

North Leigh scout group in about 1920. The skipper was Miss Doris Mason.

North Leigh scouts in the 1920s. Left to right: Edgar Porter, Harry Simister, Fred Porter, W. Limmer, Bert Breakspeare, William Wickson.

The old school interior, North Leigh.

North Leigh School group in 1930. Back row, left to right: S. Heritage, A. Arkell, F. Willis, A. Parsons, G. Bartlett, R. Langford, S. Breakspeare. Second row: V. Harris, J. Parsons, E. Cooper, P. Barrett, E. Woodward, S. Buckingham, S. Willis, P. Busby, D. Goodman. Third row: D. Parsons, M. Woodward, C. Newson, M. Souch, W. Souch, M. Green, A. Lay, E. Webb, B. Webb. Front row: R. Buckingham, L. Langford, S. Souch, H. Goodman, B. Cape, M. Northover.

Ramsden High Street in around 1910.

Ramsden High Street, looking north, in around 1910. The house in the centre of the picture was the village stores but is now a private house.

The Heythrop foxhounds meet at Ramsden House, 1935.

Ramsden Mothers Union dressed for a play, *Pandora's Box*, in around 1932. Left to right: Ms Greenaway, R. Wallace, Pimm, Wright, Wallace, Panting, Twamley, Ford, Willoughby, Beames, Fathers. Front row, seated: S. Johnson and Mrs Twamley's mother.

Ramsden Cricket Club in 1960 when they were Witney League division one cup winners. Standing, left to right: N. and R. Willoughby, R. Shirley, M. Hitchcock, P. Howse, W. Millin, G. Panting, J. Lever. Seated: P. Hitchcock, W. Slater, B. Englefield, F. Ford, J. Millin, K. Hollifield, H. Hollifield.

Ramsden celebrated the coronation of King George VI with a cricket match: married men versus single men, 12 May 1937.

Ramsden School group in around 1950. It was a Church of England school and pupils moved on to Finstock School at the age of nine.

Ramsden and Finstock baby welfare clinic in 1948. This was held in the village hall at Finstock with Doctor Crowley of Charlbury in attendance.

Wilcote Lane, Ramsden, in around 1910.

Children in fancy dress and spectators at Ramsden House for the celebrations of the coronation of King George VI, 12 May 1937.

Eynsham Hall, a large house on the outskirts of North Leigh, was demolished in 1903 and a larger house was built on the site. The new house was completed in 1908. The picture shows the men who worked on the rebuilding: C. Corderoy, C. Dore, J. Holland, A. Wharton, W. Timms, R. Horne, G. Rhymes, W. Harris, W. Buck, J. Hill, J. Rush, G. Dore, P. Ayris, J. Coullin, C. Harris, T. Cox, G. Neville, F. Hopkins, G. Sydenham, R. Cox, W. Taylor, J. Judd, A. Dunsby, W. Beckley, W. Church, A. Church, E. Neville, A. Drinkwater, M. Taylor, J. Langford, H. Cox, J. Rose, G. Bishop, F. George, F. Smith, W. Church.

Gardeners on the Eynsham Hall estate. Mr Hopkins, on the right, was the head gardener.

Estate workers and maintenance men on the Eynsham Hall estate.

Jack Groves from New Yatt was a First World War despatch rider.

Part of Jack Groves's collection of vintage cycles.

SECTION SIX

Charlbury – Spelsbury – Finstock
Shorthampton – Leafield

Pound Hill, Charlbury, on the Spelsbury Road, from a postcard dated 6 August 1909.

Spelsbury Road, Charlbury, in around 1906. A lane to the right leads to the River Evenlode, where children used to swim.

Church Street, Charlbury, around 1900, in the days of the horse-drawn vehicle. Market stalls would be set up outside the Bell Hotel and cattle pens to the rear.

Church Street, Charlbury, on 16 March 1907. Allen's drapery shop is on the right, the Royal Oak temperance hotel next door. Mr Ball, grocer, is left, then a building used as a cinema during the Second World War. The next building is Mr Andrew's fish and chip shop.

Sheep Street, Charlbury, in around 1906. The Bull Hotel is on the left, with Milton the ironmongers on the right.

The end of Sheep Street, Charlbury, leading to Hixet Wood, in around 1920. The Railway Arms public house is on the left.

Market Street, Charlbury, in around 1920. On the left is the post office before it moved further down the street; Barclays Bank occupied the next site but closed during 1992. Next came Jull, the chemist.

Warner's, later Morrison's garage in around 1920. Miss Vincent's toy shop was opposite. The Midland Bank was nearby but closed many years ago.

Market Street, Charlbury, in around 1920.

Lee Place, Charlbury, in around 1900. The small wicket gate leads to the croquet lawn.

An important glove-making industry was centred on Charlbury, Woodstock, Witney and Leafield, employing mostly women. This is one of the machine rooms, in around 1950, where component parts were stitched into gloves. Cheap imports and plastics have destroyed this industry.

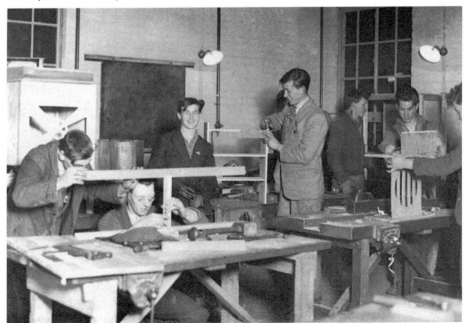

This workshop was set up in Charlbury during the 1930s to train young people. I suppose the Youth Training Scheme is the modern equivalent.

Country dancers from Ascott-under-Wychwood attend a fête at Lee Place, Charlbury, in 1925.

Knowing how long a chess match can take, one hopes these living chess pieces have plenty of patience. They are part of the entertainment at Charlbury fête held at Lee Place in 1929.

Visitors to Charlbury Flower Show, in 1935.

Spectators at Charlbury fête, held at Lee Place, in 1929. Both pictures on this page show how fashionable it was to wear a hat.

Charlbury railway station on the Oxford–Worcester line in around 1930, showing the coalyard on the left, which is now a car park, and the gasometer on the right, which was removed many years ago.

The paraffin delivery man was once a familiar sight, especially in the rural areas. These two men were delivering Pratt's Oil, a product of the Anglo American Oil Co., in Spelsbury, a village north of Charlbury.

Rangers Lodge in the Wychwood Forest, west of Charlbury, after a fire on 31 December 1921.

Manor House, Finstock, on 8 June 1906. Believed to date from the 1600s, it was the home of Mr and Mrs Bolton and their two daughters. Mrs Bolton is seen behind the wall and daughter Kathleen by the gate. John Wesley used to stay at the house.

In this 1913 photograph, Percy Hirons stands by the regulator on this Marshall portable farm engine, which was made at Gainsborough in around 1900. It generated the power for farm work at Shorthampton Farm near Charlbury.

St Michael and all Angels church, Leafield, as seen from the green in the 1930s. One of the original water supply points, used before individual properties had their own supply, is still to be seen at the side of the end property.

Leafield church, 1918. The village hut on the right is made of wood. It was given to the village by Mr George Yapp, and has been used for dances and social occasions. It is now held in trust.

Leafield church spire had to be rebuilt in 1865. In 1934 the spire was shortened after the top third had been removed and rebuilt. The lychgate was erected by Mr Watney in 1920 as a First World War memorial.

The opening ceremony of Leafield water supply in around 1926. Water was pumped from Shipton-under-Wychwood to standpipes at several points in the village. Mr Watney, the Lord of the Manor, gives a brief history of the village.

Miss Pearce, teacher, and schoolchildren in front of the newly erected council houses, Fairspear Road, Leafield, in around 1926.

A typical summer scene in the 1920s. The type of cart suggests that this three-horse team was busy transporting the harvest from field to rickyard.

Road repairing on the Burford–Chipping Norton road in 1923. This was hard, labour intensive work and the only mechanical assistance was from the steam road roller.

Mr Hewett, the baker, on Leafield Green, on his delivery round.

Mr and Mrs Loxton driving their pride and joy, a three-wheeler, registration no. AE2100.

Leafield Football Club, in 1932/3 when they won the Woodstock charity cup and the Milton-under-Wychwood and British Legion six-a-side cup. Mr Hewett, the baker, stands on the right.

Probably under the guidance of the Revd Lee, who was vicar of Leafield, these young members of the Girls Friendly Society are on a visit to Chipping Norton. The fashions suggest that the date is around 1900.

Leafield 1st Company of girl guides in 1927.

The Revd Caleb Nightingale, right, and his party of volunteers, ready to clean Leafield church, in 1928.

Leafield School group in 1926.

The church Sunday school summer outing to the seaside sometime in the 1930s. They usually chose Southsea or Weston. There would be several of Back's coaches and most of the villagers would go.

First World War soldiers parade on the green at Leafield. They guarded the radio station at nearby Langley.

The radio station guard march along the Fairspeare Road. Their parent unit was probably the RASC stationed at Witney in large numbers during the war.

A fête at Leafield in 1925, proceeds of which were for the national children's homes and orphanage.

The Revd Caleb Nightingale of Leafield and visitors at a garden fête, on August Bank Holiday Monday 1927. Apparently it was a wet day as it so often is for English summer outdoor events.

The first Saturday after Whit Sunday was club day at Leafield, a day of festivities when there was a share out of monies that had been paid in throughout the year. This photograph shows the 1911 celebrations.

Club day parade behind the banners of the various Leafield public houses in 1929. This was a day of fun and drinking, sometimes ending with fights on the village green.

SECTION SEVEN

Ascott-under-Wychwood
Shipton-under-Wychwood – Bruern
Milton-under-Wychwood

Ascott-under-Wychwood, as seen from London Lane. The school, situated on the green, can be seen on the left.

The entrance to Ascott-under-Wychwood from the level crossing. The Churchill Arms on the left was later renamed Wychwood Arms, but has now been converted for residential use.

Ascott-under-Wychwood High Street and the village shop.

A house on the village green which is now partly used as a garage. On the green is a seat commemorating sixteen Ascott women martyrs who were gaoled in 1873 for the part they played in protecting their husbands' jobs on the farms after a wages dispute.

Ascott-under-Wychwood station, level crossing and station building.

The Oxford–Worcester railway line passes through Ascott-under-Wychwood. Here gangers repair the track.

Ascott-under-Wychwood School as seen from the green. It closed in around 1989, but was not empty for long as the Windrush private school from Burford relocated to it.

Ascott-under-Wychwood School group in around 1913.

Ascott-under-Wychwood School group in around 1940.

Ascott-under-Wychwood School group in around 1924.

Ascott-under-Wychwood Lifeboys at Aldwick near Bognor Regis for their summer camp, in August 1934.

Ascott-under-Wychwood branch of the Workers' Educational Association, 1913.

Ascott-under-Wychwood nursing association fête, 28 July 1923.

The opening ceremony of the church fête at the vicarage, Ascott-under-Wychwood, on 10 July 1926. It was declared open by the Countess of Eltham.

Children at play on the green, Ascott-under-Wychwood, June 1922.

Ascott-under-Wychwood football team, 1922/3 season.

Ascott-under-Wychwood folk dancing club, which included morris dancers, in 1920.

The Heythrop foxhounds meet on Ascott-under-Wychwood village green, Easter Monday 1934.

The Crown Inn, or Shaven Crown as it is now called, Shipton-under-Wychwood, in 1826.

The shop and post office in Church Street, opposite the Crown Inn, Shipton-under-Wychwood, before 1930.

The Red Horse public house, Shipton-under-Wychwood. Hunt Edmund, the supplying brewer, was at Banbury. This brewery was taken over by a larger company and is now controlled by Charringtons. The Banbury brewery was pulled down and the central site redeveloped.

Station Road, Shipton-under-Wychwood. The flood, in February 1933, followed a thaw after heavy snowfall which caused the River Evenlode to overflow.

Originally a college for young ladies, St Michael's in Shipton-under-Wychwood has been a home for waifs and strays, accommodation for Basque refugees, a billet for troops 1939–45, a corn chandlery and 'Ye Olde Junk Shop'. It was demolished in 1989 and the site redeveloped.

Princess Victoria of Schleswig-Holstein and the Revd W.C. Carter on a visit to see the waifs and strays in the house shown above. The princess was staying at Bruern Abbey, Shipton-under-Wychwood.

A peep into the United Woodwork Co. workshop, where wooden cash tills were made.

Employees of the United Woodwork Co., at the factory in Station Road, Shipton-under-Wychwood. The company ceased trading in 1971.

Boys from Shipton, Ascott and Milton with their master, Mr Horne, at Shipton-under-Wychwood School. This is the gardening class, photographed on the occasion of the Jubilee of King George V, 6 May 1935.

The same class of boys, photographed at the same time.

During the 1930s the Conservative Party organized summer fêtes at large houses around the county. In this picture the VIPs sit on a dais while the speeches are made at Shipton Court. The member of parliament for this area at the time was Major James Edmunson; he can be seen between the two sunshades, leaning on his cane.

Fancy dress at Shipton-under-Wychwood church fête, 1925.

Mr Dee built his shop near to the village green at Shipton-under-Wychwood in 1919; he left in the early 1930s. It is still a grocery shop. The photograph shows his family ready for an outing in 1921.

Mr Joe Griffin and his men making hay at Hill Farm, Bruern, in 1921. Griffin also farmed and lived at Bruern Grange.

Milton-under-Wychwood Mothers Union outside Frogmore House in around 1900.

Quarrymen who worked for Mr Groves in the Milton-under-Wychwood stone quarry, in around 1900.

SECTION EIGHT

Minster Lovell – Worsham
Asthall and Asthall Leigh – Swinbrook

Lower Minster Lovell, a very pretty village on the edge of the Cotswolds, in the 1930s.

Lower Minster Lovell, slightly nearer to the ruined manor house, in the late 1930s.

Charterville allotments in Minster Lovell was the brainchild of the eccentric Irish politician Fergus O'Connor. He purchased 300 acres of land for his pet agricultural scheme. The picture shows one of the bungalows which was built. Each plot contained from 2½ to 4 acres and had its own well.

The bridge over the River Windrush, in 1940, showing the house which has long since disappeared. The field beyond the road is now the recreation ground, having been bequeathed to the village by Mrs A.W. De Sales LaTerrier.

Minster Lovell's old toll-house on the right and Mrs Dale's Toll House Café on the left, in around 1936. The café is now a private house.

In July 1956 a road-widening scheme was started in Minster Lovell, and here the workmen are removing slates from the toll-house as the first stage of demolition. The White Hart public house can be seen in the centre distance.

The interior of the Toll House Café. In the summer Witney people would walk to Minster Lovell, have tea at the café and walk back by the River Windrush in the valley. Mrs Dale opened her café in 1936.

Ye Olde Swan, Minster Lovell, is believed to date to the fifteenth century. This postcard is dated 16 August 1937. The public house is now a popular country hotel.

Members of the Witney Urban and Rural District Councils and other notabilities attend the laying of the foundation stone of the new water extraction and purification building at Worsham on the River Windrush, 2 October 1936.

I wonder how many hats were lost from the open charabanc during this day outing to Southsea in around 1924. The trip started at Asthall Leigh.

Asthall Parish Cricket Club. The team won the Witney and District second division cup in 1935.

Asthall School group in around 1917.

Two intrepid motorcyclists from Asthall, probably photographed some time between 1914 and 1918. Sam Walker is on the right. Note the streamlining: hats worn backwards.

A typical country scene at Asthall in 1945. The occasion is the birthday of farmer Sam Walker, fifth from the left in the front row, for whom this day's shooting had been arranged.

The second Baron Redesdale at Asthall Manor, *c*. 1920, before his family moved to its new house at Swinbrook in 1926. Left and right: Lady Redesdale, Lord Redesdale. Back row: Nancy, Tom (who was killed in the Second World War). Middle row: Diana, Pamela. Front row: Unity, Jessica, Deborah.

Rick-making at Swinbrook. The elevator is being used to transport the sheaves of wheat to the top of the rick.

Carter Haines with his horse-drawn plough at Flats Farm, Swinbrook.

The cinema heart-throb in 1934 was an English actor named Anthony Bushell. He was the star of a film called *Lilies of the Field* which was made at Swinbrook. This photograph of the film being shot was taken outside the Swan public house.

Swinbrook cricket team in 1923 when they were winners of the Witney and District second division cup. Back row, left to right: R. Wilkins, F. Ilott, F. Johnson, C. Temple, H. Walker, J. Walker, J. Clarke, C. Temple. Front row: J. Walker, Darkie Arnold, Illingworth, W. Lye, C. Kinchin.

Acknowledgements

This book covers forty-two communities so I have sought assistance in the form of loaned pictures or information from a large number of people.

I would like to specially mention Mr R. Barratt for having spent many hours in his darkroom producing hundreds of photographic prints. Thanks, Roy. And a sincere thank you to all whose names I list below for their unstinted kindness, without which the production of this book would not have been possible:

Mrs M. Beckinsale • Mr C. Bustin • Mrs J. Buttrick • Mr R. Buxton
Mr A. Clarke • Mr H. Clarke • Mr K. Cook • Mr R. Cripps
Mr J. Dosset Davies • Mrs J. Eeles • Mr B. Elliott • Mr R. Empson
Mrs J. Faulkner • Mrs M. Fidler • Mrs P. Finlayson • Miss C. Fitzgerald
Mr G. Fowler • Mr W. Gasson • Mrs G. Glanville • Mrs A. Hatt
Mr & Mrs J. Hirons • Mrs H. Hunt • Mr M. Linfield • Mrs K. Long
Mr P. MacGreggor • Mr G. Panting • Miss J. Pocock • Mr & Mrs B. Pullen
Ramsden WI members • Miss P. Ranssom • Mr J. Rawlins • Miss E. Read
Mr J. Read • Mr D. Rose • Mrs C. Smith • Mrs J. Snelgrove • Mr K. Southam
Mr J. Stenning • Mr & Mrs G. Steptoe • Mr A. Stevens • Mrs R. Stockhill
Miss S. Stone • Mrs J. Sutton • Mr G. Swinford • Mrs M. Tinner
Mr W. Townsend • Mrs M. Viner • Mr C. Walker • Mrs J. Walker
Mrs M. Walker • Mrs C. Warner • Mrs W. Wiggins • Mr & Mrs F. Wilkinson
Mr G. Woodley